DRUGS AND DRIVING

Drug use is one of the most common causes of serious traffic accidents.

THE DRUG ABUSE PREVENTION LIBRARY

DRUGS AND DRIVING

Janet Grosshandler

THE ROSEN PUBLISHING GROUP, INC.

NEW YORK

Published in 1992, 1994, 1998 by The Rosen Publishing Group, Inc.
29 East 21st Street, New York, NY 10010

Revised Edition 1998

Library of Congress Cataloging-in-Publication Data

Grosshandler, Janet.
    Drugs and driving / Janet Grosshandler.
      (The drug abuse prevention library)
    Includes bibliographical references and index.
    Summary: Discusses the use of drugs by teenagers, and in particular, the consequences of combining drugs and driving.
    ISBN 0-8239-2616-8
    1. Automobile drivers—United States—Drug use—Juvenile literature. [1. Automobile drivers—Drug use. 2. Drug abuse 3. Drinking and traffic accidents. 4. Traffic accidents.]
    I. Title. II. Series.
    HE5620.D65G76 1992, 1994
    363.1'251—dc21   92-6146
                                             CIP
                                           AC

Manufactured in the United States of America

Contents

Chapter 1   It Could Be You: Tom's Story   7

Chapter 2   Overview   *11*

Chapter 3   What Drugs Do to You   *16*

Chapter 4   Facts About a Growing Problem   *29*

Chapter 5   What Can Drugs Do to a Driver's Skills?   *35*

Chapter 6   But I'm Not a Criminal! Drugs and the Law   *42*

Chapter 7   Tragic Results   *49*

Chapter 8   What You Can Do   *53*

Glossary—*Explaining New Words*   *59*

Where to Go for Help   *61*

For Further Reading   *62*

Index   *63*

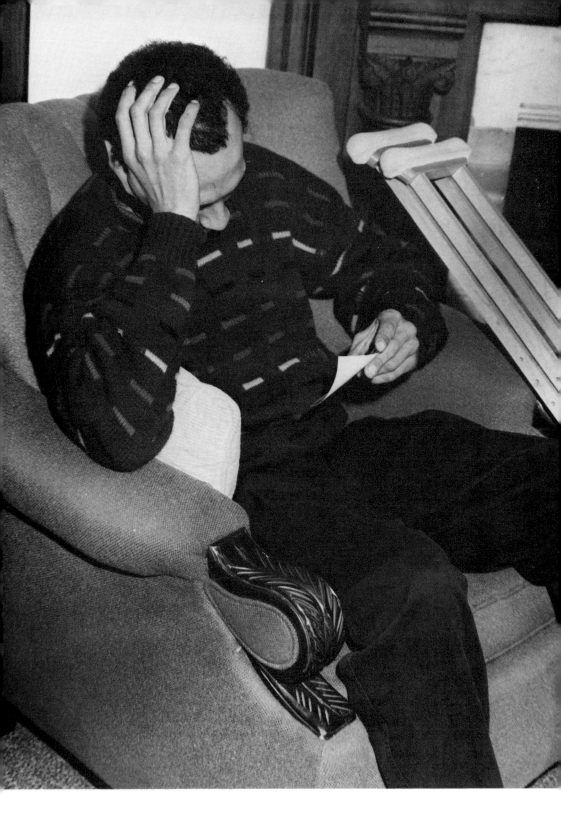

Being responsible for the death of a friend is a heavy burden.

CHAPTER 1

It Could Be You: Tom's Story

"I never thought it could happen to me." That's what Tom has to say now. And now he knows how wrong he was.

Every weekend Tom and his friends hit the local party scene. They'd have a few beers, smoke a couple of joints, and cruise around. Sounds pretty normal, right? But this Saturday was different.

"My folks let me take the car out, and I had to swear I'd be home by 1 a.m. I picked up my girlfriend, Melissa, and drove to Dave's, where he was having a keg party. Melissa and her friends didn't want to stay long, so I said okay. But I wanted to get a good buzz before I left, because otherwise what's the point? I downed a few brews

8 and took a hit of grass, and I was feeling pretty good. Some of the guys were doing acid, but I never went in for any of that hard stuff. I just wanted to relax a little, you know?

"In a little while, Melissa said she wanted to go. She asked me if I was okay to drive, and I started giving her this "macho" speech about how I could handle my beer. I'll never forget how she asked me if I should really be driving. Why didn't I listen? I guess I was more wasted than I thought. Anyway, we backed out of the driveway and went down Dave's street to the corner where you turn left onto the four-lane. I didn't really stop at the stop sign because it was the middle of the night and I couldn't see any cars. I didn't look too close, I guess, because the next thing I remember there's this van speeding up from the right. Actually that's the last thing I remember about that night."

Tom didn't wake up for three weeks. He was in a coma all that time from hitting his head on the windshield. He's been in physical therapy for the last year. Melissa and the driver of the van, an elderly man, weren't so lucky. They were both killed immediately upon impact, crushed when

the van collided with Tom's car. Neither of **9**
them ever had a chance.

*Tom doesn't take driving and driving
lightly anymore. He has been convicted of
two counts of manslaughter. He has to pay
$30,000 in fines and serve 10 years of community service. And worst of all, he has to
live with the guilt because he thought he
was too cool to admit he was drunk.*

*"I guess the message I most want to tell
people is that it is just not worth it. I can
never forgive myself for causing Melissa's
death or the death of that old man, who was
just driving down the street. I try to keep
my friends away from cars if they've been
drinking or doing drugs. You just never
know what can happen. Believe me, it can
happen to anybody."*

Hundreds of thousands of people are killed or injured in drug-related car accidents each year.

CHAPTER 2

Overview

*A*merican teenagers are killing others and themselves at an alarming rate in car crashes. Drugged drivers kill themselves and thousands of innocent people by getting behind the wheel when they are high.

Each year, hundreds of thousands of people are maimed, scarred, paralyzed, burned, and killed in these accidents. The numbers average out to about one person every minute of every day. When you get into a car, your chances of being in an accident are one in seven. When you get into a car a little bit high or with a drugged driver, your chances rise to one in three. Are those the kinds of odds you want to bet your life on?

12 Alcohol is the drug that gets the most publicity because it is the drug that teens use most often. However, it is not the only drug that can affect your ability to drive. Using marijuana, cocaine, crack, amphetamines, and barbiturates makes you a menace on the highway. Drugs blur your vision and affect your reflexes, coordination, and judgement.

Some over-the-counter medicines can affect your driving ability, too. Sleeping pills, cough medicines, allergy pills, and cold remedies may contain amphetamines which can interfere with your driving. Read the labels on medicine bottles you have at home. A lot of them contain alcohol and carry warnings not to drive or operate machinery when using them. These medicines may also cause drowsiness, sleeplessness, nervousness, and irritability. If you are taking one of them, your ability to drive can be impaired. And if you combine it with a few beers, you can be arrested for DUI (driving under the influence).

Any drug, including alcohol, can interfere with your ability to make safe judgements, your vision, and your driving skills.

Eighty percent (eight out of ten) of fatal accidents are first accidents. To say, "I've never had a single accident," is no excuse to take driving lightly. The statistics show that teenagers are at huge risk for accidents because they don't have years of experience with driving. They certainly can't handle driving while high on drugs. Too many teens and young adults kill themselves and others because they mix drugs and driving.

In addition to the terrible sadness brought to families when one member is involved in a car crash, the financial costs of drugged driving are staggering. Medical expenses, property damage, court costs, lawyers' fees, and time lost from school or work can soar to hundreds of thousands of dollars for *each* accident.

If you are arrested and convicted of drugged driving, you face time in jail, fines of hundreds or thousands of dollars, community service, loss of your driver's license, and possibly cancellation of insurance. If you cause a death or serious injuries in an accident or are involved in more than once accident, you could be charged with a felony. That means you face a prison sentence on conviction.

Leading Causes of Death (15–24 Year Olds)

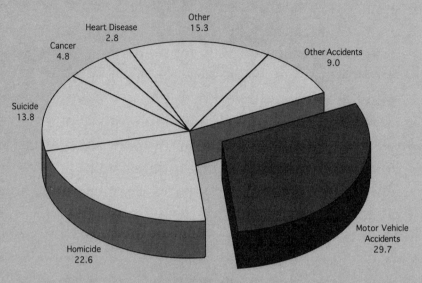

Heart Disease
2.8

Other
15.3

Cancer
4.8

Other Accidents
9.0

Suicide
13.8

Motor Vehicle
Accidents
29.7

Homicide
22.6

Rate per 100,000

Source: U.S. Department of Health and Human Services, 1994 statistics

- In America, over one million people suffer serious injuries every year because of drunk and drugged drivers.
- About two in every five Americans will be involved in an alcohol-related crash at some time in their lives.
- Between 1984 and 1993, the number of people arrested for drunkenness who were under 18 years old increased by 42.9 percent; for DUI it increased by 50.2 percent and for drug abuse it increased by 27.8 percent.
- In 1995, 17,274 people died in alcohol-related crashes—that's about one death every 30 minutes.

More teenagers are dying from car accidents than from anything else. One of the major contributors to these accidents is the use of drugs, including alcohol.

Driving is one of the first big steps you take toward becoming an adult. Getting your license means freedom—and new independence.

Alcohol and other drugs can give you a false sense of control. Because drugs can alter a person's perception, a drunk or drugged driver will not realize how dangerously he or she is driving. These drivers may not know that they are driving too fast or too slow. Many drugs slow your reaction time. People driving under the influence of these drugs do not realize that they cannot make quick decisions. Drugs can make your senses so dulled that you are not able to make clear judgments. People may believe that they are still able to drive a car, even though they are drunk or have taken drugs. But driving in this condition will put their lives and the lives of others in great danger.

CHAPTER 3

What Drugs Do to You

*T*he things you put into your body will affect the way it functions. For example, eating nutritious foods will make your body healthier than it would be if you ate lots of junk foods.

Alcohol and drugs can have damaging effects on your body. Over time, alcohol addiction can cause serious medical problems, including cirrhosis, a disease of the liver. Overdoses of alcohol and many other drugs can be fatal. Despite these dangers, drug and alcohol use remain major problems among teens. One study shows that at least 15 percent of students between 12 and 17 years old have serious alcohol or drug problems. Five percent of teens who get involved with alcohol or drugs will eventually develop an addiction.

Everything you put into your body affects you. Taking care of
yourself means eating nutritious foods that help you feel good.

18 People often start using drugs believing that they will not become addicted. But the number of addicts shows that it is easy for a person to lose control of his or her drug use. Drugs have powerful physical and emotional controls over the body. Once a person is addicted, he or she will feel severely depressed or sick without the drug. Recovering will be a long and difficult process.

Alcohol is the most commonly abused drug among teens *and* adults. When it enters the bloodstream, it is sent to all parts of the body. Your reflexes, coordination, memory, and judgment all undergo changes. A person who is drunk can have slurred speech, double vision, experience mood swings, and even become unconscious.

Excessive drinking can kill you. Hundreds of college students die from alcohol poisoning every year. But many people still do not know how harmful alcohol can be. A study by The Center for Substance Abuse and Prevention revealed that 2.6 million teens don't realize that a person can die from an alcohol overdose.

Drunk driving is a major problem all over the United States. The National

Highway Traffic Safety Association
reported that more than half of all teen
auto accidents are caused by drunk driving. In 1995, 2,200 teen drivers died in
alcohol-related traffic accidents. In fact,
one teen dies in an alcohol-related car
crash every 3 hours. It is likely that
everyone knows or has heard about
someone in their school, town, or city
who has become a victim of drunk
driving.

Hallucinogens are drugs that change
your ability to sense what is real or unreal. The illusion that you experience
may range from feeling "high" or
euphoric (like being detached or free-
floating) to seeing, hearing, and sensing
things that are not really there.

Marijuana (also called "pot," "grass,"
"reefer," "smoke," "weed," or "shake") is
a hallucinogen that contains a com-
pound called THC. The THC is absorbed
into your lungs, brain, and liver. It can
stay in your body for days, and can
cause a great deal of damage.

Smoking marijuana can damage your
lungs and impair brain functions such
as thinking, learning, and remembering.
It can make you feel insecure or fright-

Alcohol and nicotine are addictive substances that can pose a risk to your health.

ened, uninterested and uncaring, or even paranoid (suspicious and afraid). Even though pot used to be thought of as "harmless," current research suggests that it is a dangerous drug. For many young people, it is the first illegal drug they try after using the legal drugs tobacco and alcohol.

Another hallucinogen is phencyclidine, known as PCP or angel dust. In small doses, PCP has effects like those of alcohol: poor coordination, slurred speech, mental confusion, sleepiness, and numbness in fingers and toes. Users may also tend to feel nauseated and may

vomit.

In large doses, PCP can act like an anesthetic, a drug used to put people to sleep before an operation. Your senses may be disturbed or blocked. You may feel left out, alone, and isolated. Some people have felt these effects last up to ten days.

PCP can also cause terrible depression, severe mental suffering, or flashbacks. People have died from PCP.

LSD, or acid, is another hallucinogen. Even in tiny doses, LSD cause the pupils of your eyes to dilate, your blood pressure to rise, your heart to beat irregularly, and the muscles of your internal organs to contract. At first, the effects are slow and mild, but then the hallucinations start. You "see" sounds or "hear" colors.

An acid trip jumbles the real and unreal images and feelings. It can quickly turn into a horror show, and the user can be driven into a state of violent behavior. The effects of LSD can last for hours. Much later, inactive parts of the drug that remain in your body can become active again, and you may have another LSD trip against your will. That is a flashback, and it can haunt you for a long time.

22   Using PCP or LSD will alter your brain—in some cases permanently.

Stimulant drugs speed up the activities of the cells in the central nervous system. Caffeine found in coffee, tea, and cola, and the nicotine found in cigarettes are examples of stimulants that occur naturally in plants.

Other stimulants are human-made. They are called amphetamines and are used to treat certain illnesses. Abusing amphetamines can lead to dependency. Many states have declared them illegal, except for medical purposes.

Amphetamines are usually made in the form of capsules, tablets, or powder. Some people mix amphetamines with heroin to try to get a longer high. This can sometimes be fatal.

Amphetamines affect your body by speeding up your heart rate and other body functions. You feel excitable, and your speech is fast and unclear. You are restless, and your hands shake. You may perspire and experience sleeplessness.

A user may experience other effects such as nervousness, memory lapse, irritability, or hallucination. Headache, dizziness, and blurred vision are also possible.

Even though alcohol is a legal drug, responsible teenagers know
its dangers and turn it down.

24   The drug cocaine is sometimes called a superstimulant, even though it is classified as a narcotic. Cocaine may be snorted or injected. It acts immediately on the central nervous system. Your pulse rate and respiration increase. Your body temperature and blood pressure rise. When the drug reaches your bloodstream you feel a "rush," a high that may last half an hour.

People have different reactions to cocaine. Some feel energetic, others say they can think more clearly. These reactions are short-lived. Many users experience depression when the effects of cocaine wear off. Heavy users often become more aggressive and anxious. Mood swings and memory losses have also been reported. Habitual "coke" users may experience convulsions and some become paralyzed.

"Crack" is the street name given to a form of cocaine that is smoked. It looks like shavings or slivers of soap. Crack is sold in small bottles, in folding papers, or in heavy tinfoil. It is usually smoked in a pipe. Crack is an extremely addictive drug.

Solvents are volatile substances that people sniff or inhale. Glue, airplane glue, lighter fluid, nail-polish remover, cleaning fluids, and gasoline are commonly abused. Solvents are mainly abused by children ranging in age from 8 to 16.

Some of the signs and symptoms of glue sniffing are a runny nose, chemical odor on the breath and clothes, double vision, foul breath, watering eyes, staggering walk, slurred speech, and drowsiness. Periodic violent acts against themselves are also traits of glue sniffers.

Safe driving requires a clear head and sound judgment.

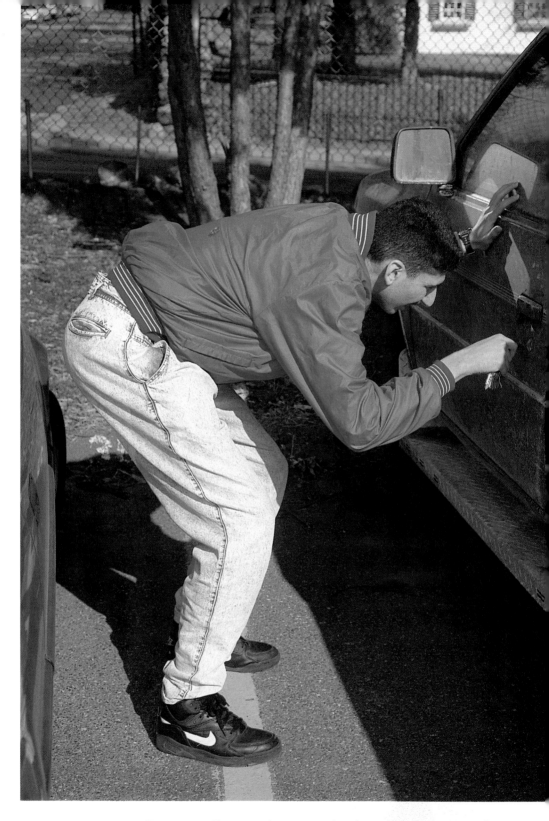

Drugs can affect coordination and make simple tasks impossible.

Young people who sniff glue may start to use other dangerous household chemicals in search of a better high. Regularly inhaling solvents can damage your brain and heart.

Narcotics are drugs that cause sleep or sluggishness as well as relieve pain. These drugs usually come from opium. Codeine and morphine are sometimes used by hospitals to treat people when they are sick. All narcotics that come from opium or are human-made, like Demerol, can be addictive if abused. That means that your body always craves more of the drug. These drugs slow down your respiratory system. Your oxygen intake can become so low that you die.

Heroin is a narcotic that can be taken in several ways. In pure powder form, it can be smoked, snorted into the nose through a straw or rolled-up dollar bill, "skin popped" (injected just under the skin), or "mainlined" (injecting directly into the vein). It is one of the most addictive drugs on earth.

Getting involved with narcotics is a losing game. Your body builds up a tolerance, and you need to use more drugs to feed your craving for the high.

28

Sedatives are other drugs that affect the central nervous system. But instead of speeding it up like stimulants, sedatives depress or slow body activities such as breathing, blood pressure, heartbeat, and cell function.

Barbiturates are sedatives that are used to treat some medical problem or to make people sleep. They are often used to relax some patients before and during surgery. Unfortunately, these drugs seem to be over prescribed because they tranquilize the user. They can become habit-forming.

If you take barbiturates, your reactions and responses are slowed, your speech is slurred and mixed up, and you feel sluggish. Your thinking becomes muddled, and your behavior may be up and down. An overdose can cause death.

All of the above descriptions are brief. But make no mistake, books can be written about each drug and its dangers. If you become involved with any of these drugs, you take risks with all aspects of your life—your health, your mental stability, your family, your relationships, your present and your future, for as long as you *have* a future.

CHAPTER 4

Facts About a Growing Problem

*T*hink about these facts:
- 42 percent of teen deaths were the result of alcohol-related accidents.
- Almost 11 percent of people between 12 and 17 years old have used an illegal drug.
- In 1996, one in four high school sophomores and one third of the seniors reported to have had five or more alcoholic drinks, at one occasion, within the past two weeks.
- Young people account for 7 percent of the driving population, but are responsible for 12 percent of fatal crashes.
- By the time they graduate from high school, 10 percent of teens will have tried LSD.

30

- The average age for first smoking cigarettes is 11; for drinking alcohol, 12;
and for smoking marijuana, 13.
- A federal government survey on drug
abuse found that 12,823,000 people
admitted to using an illegal drug
within the month of the survey.
- In 1995, the number of eighth graders
who had used marijuana, cocaine, and
LSD was the highest it had ever been
in the United States. One study shows
that 15.8 percent of people interviewed
had used marijuana in the last year, 2.6
percent had used cocaine, and 3.2 percent had used LSD.

Going with the Crowd

"I can sit in homeroom on a Monday
morning," said Jemal, 17, "and hear about
who drank what and who snorted what at
all the weekend parties. No one tries to
keep it a secret anymore. Kids in my
school are bragging about being wasted."

"In my crowd," said Les, 16, "probably 80 to 90 percent of the kids drink a
couple of weekends a month. There's not
much else to do, I guess. Last week some
of the guys were doing acid, but not
everyone wanted to try it."

Many "legal" over-the-counter drugs can affect driving ability.
Always read warning labels.

Letting a friend drive if you have had alcohol is the responsible thing to do.

Depending on your crowd, your
friends may not drink, may drink once
in a while, or they may drink often and
push drinking as a requirement to stay
in the crowd. The decisions you make
about whether or not to put drugs or
alcohol in your body can affect many
aspects of your life—acceptance by your
peers, dealings with your parents, sexual
relationships, your health, schoolwork,
run-ins with the police, and more.

Most teenage passenger deaths occur
when another teen is driving. In 1995,
3,237 teen drivers (16 to 20 years old)
were killed in traffic crashes and 2,088
were passengers.

The fatality rate for teenage drivers,
based on estimated annual travel, is
about four times as high as the rate for
drivers 25 to 65 years old. That's a
sobering fact when you consider that
there are probably more older drivers on
the road than there are teenagers. Do
the statistics tell us that teenagers are
less responsible than adults? Does it
prove that they are more reckless? What
can be done to prevent the dangers of
drinking and driving among young
people?

34   A survey of high-school seniors reported that the percentage of drivers having
one or more moving violations (running
a stop sign or a red light, speeding, etc.)
in a 12-month period went up by almost
7 percent from 1982 to 1987. Almost 5
percent reported having been ticketed
for a moving violation after using alcohol
in the same 12 months. In total, the survey
indicated that more than 36 percent of
those high-school seniors who were ticketed or arrested for moving violations
were driving under the influence.

"My friends and I were stopped a few
weeks ago," said José, 16. "The cop asked
if we had been drinking and we said no.
Then he gave Brad a speeding ticket and
let us go. And we were pretty drunk. So
maybe there's even more of that going on."

Statistics are not always 100 percent
right. But if the above information is 80
or 90 percent correct, it still is too many
kids getting high, drunk, hurt, and killed
on the road.

CHAPTER 5

What Can Drugs Do to a Driver's Skills?

*A*fter the party, Alex offered to drive his friends home. As the designated driver, he didn't drink any alcohol. His best friend, Dave, sat in the passenger seat, flipping from one radio station to the next. The music blared. Alex started to speed.

Out of the corner of his eye, Alex saw a car pulling up beside his. Without signaling, the car changed lanes, cutting directly in front. Alex slammed on the brakes just in time. He honked the horn. Luckily, Alex and Dave had their seat belts on. Stunned, everyone in the car quieted. The other car drove off ahead. Dave shut off the radio. Alex could feel his heart pounding. If he reacted one second later, he would have hit the other car.

36   But how might this scenario have turned out if Alex had been drinking and driving?

Alex drove home, dropping off friends along the way. He had several drinks at the party, but he felt like he was in control. His best friend, Dave, was in the passenger seat, flipping from one radio station to the next. The music blared. Alex had started to speed and did not notice that he ran a stop sign.

Alex also didn't see that a car pulled up next to his. Without signaling, the car changed lanes, cutting directly in front of him. Alex took too long to figure out what was happening. He tried to step on the brake, but it was too late. He slammed into the car in front of him.

Drugs interfere with many skills that a person needs to be a safe driver.

Reaction time is how quickly you respond to something that happens. Slamming on your brakes, pulling to the side of the road to avoid hitting a car, honking your horn—all take a split second to do. Drugs like alcohol and barbiturates slow down your ability to make decisions. You can't react in the split second it takes to avoid an accident.

A good driver must be able to react quickly to unexpected situations.

38

Eye focus is important when you drive. Stop signs, traffic signs, and people on the side of the road will appear as you drive. Seeing everything clearly is a requirement. You have to pass a vision test to get your license. When you drive after doing drugs you can't focus or see clearly.

Peripheral vision is the ability to see things that are not right in front of you. Billboards, houses, other cars, and street signs pass on both sides when you are cruising down the street. You need to be able to see when a car pulls out of a driveway or intersection, or when the car next to you pulls up to change lanes.

A study was done to test how alcohol affects peripheral vision. A person with a blood-alcohol content (BAC) of .55 (that's only one or two drinks in two hours for some people) loses almost one third of peripheral vision on a field-of-vision test.

Your speed also affects peripheral vision. The faster you go, the less you are able to see things on the side. People sometimes feel "up" from a drug, have a false sense of confidence, and are not afraid to drive fast. When you speed while feeling the effects of a drug, you'll see very little except a blurry scene right in front of you.

Time-sharing skill is the ability to pay attention to several things at the same time. When you are driving, your brain must react to all the things you see in front of you. Drugs and alcohol make it more difficult to pay attention to several things at once.

Drunk drivers are not able to have the concentration it takes to put together all the information people need when they drive. All your attention and skills are needed to be a safe driver, and even the best drivers may be involved in accidents that are not their fault. If you add the effects of drugs, drivers are more easily distracted, no matter how skilled they may be when sober. Drugs will impair the time-sharing skills you need to drive safely and increase the odds of having an accident.

Night vision is your ability to see when it is dark. Driving at night requires even more caution and concentration. This is because at night, your vision can be reduced by as much as half. Taking drugs, especially alcohol, reduces the oxygen in your bloodstream, which affects your vision. Then you drive with even less night vision than when you are sober.

Night driving takes extra concentration because vision is greatly reduced.

Any drug is a mind-altering substance. **41**
When you combine drugs, the effects are
increased. Certain drugs may make you
feel stimulated. You feel flushed. Your
heart beats faster, and you lose some of
your inhibitions. You feel freer to talk,
laugh, and act carelessly. You are more
likely to take risks. Things that would
normally seem scary or dangerous suddenly seem easier and less stressful.

Drunk drivers often take dangerous
risks because the alcohol keeps them
from being cautious. When people are
drunk, they are unable to judge the consequences of their actions.

Too many people think that they are
able to drive after drinking at a party.
Believing that your driving skills remain
good when you are drunk or high is
common. In one study, drunk drivers
knocked over orange cones and ran
down flags, but they still thought they
drove as well as they did when they
were sober. To be a safe driver and
reduce your chances of accidents, you
need to be alert, sharp, and in control.
Drugs interfere with your brain, your
emotions, your coordination, and every
skill you need to drive.

CHAPTER 6

But I'm Not a Criminal! Drugs and the Law

*I*f you drive under the influence of drugs, you are a criminal. That may not seem fair, but think about it. A person who is high doesn't have the mental and physical control you need to drive a car. And a car that isn't in control can become a lethal weapon at any moment. The laws against DWI (Driving While Intoxicated) and DUI (Driving Under the Influence) are there to protect innocent people from getting hurt or killed by a driver who's not in control.

If You Are Pulled Over
If you are pulled over because a cop suspects you of DUI, you will be asked to do some things to determine whether you are drunk. Your blood-alcohol content (BAC)

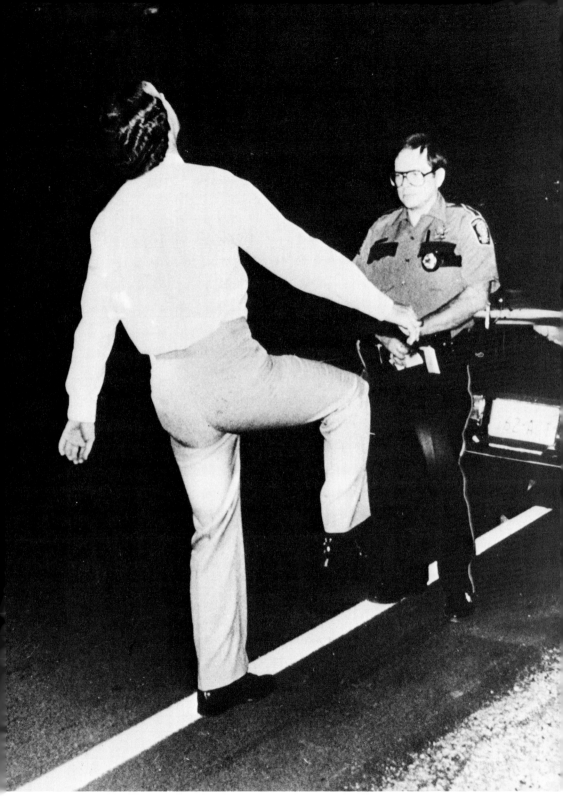

Drunken driving is a crime. Failure to pass a "sobriety" test may
lead to arrest.

44 will be tested with a Breathalyzer. You may also have to take a coordination test, doing things like walking a straight line, touching your nose, or reciting tongue-twisters. If you refuse to cooperate, your license can be suspended for 30 days. This may seem severe, but it is the way the police try to keep the roads free of drunk drivers.

If your breath measures .10 or higher on the Breathalyzer, you are legally drunk or intoxicated. In some states a reading between .05 and .10 means that you are legally impaired. You could then be taken to a hospital for urine and blood tests.

But what if the Breathalyzer says that you are not drunk from alcohol, yet other drugs have impaired your ability to drive a vehicle? For a long time the police had no legal way to test if the person they stopped was high on drugs. But the problem of combining drugs with driving has become so big that new ways are being developed to screen for drug use in drivers. A federal program called Drug Recognition is now in use, and many state and local police officers are being carefully trained to test suspected drugged drivers.

If you are suspected of driving while | **45**
high, you may be taken to a trained Drug
Recognition tester, who will put you
through tests to see if you're clean. You'll
be tested for such things as the reaction
of your pupils to light, the speed of your
pulse, quivering eyelids, bloodshot eyes,
muscle rigidity (from PCP use), and
needle scars. The recognition tests cover
seven categories of drugs: (1) central
nervous system depressants (like alcohol);
(2) stimulants (cocaine, amphetamines);
(3) hallucinogens (LSD); (4) narcotics
(heroin, Demerol, codeine); (5) PCP and
similar drugs; (6) marijuana and hashish;
and (7) inhalants (glue, etc.).

Conviction

If you are convicted in court of DUI,
you'll pay heavily for it. And if you are
found to be both drunk and high, you
can be convicted of two separate crimes
at once. The punishment for driving
while using illegal drugs is much stricter
than for driving drunk.

Fines. The laws differ in each state. In
California, for instance, you will pay a
fine of $1,000 In addition, there will be
penalty fees that can amount to an

46 additional $1,950. And that's just for your first offense.

Jail. In states such as Washington, there's a minimum of 24 consecutive hours that you'll be stuck in jail, and a maximum period of one year.

Seizure of vehicle. For a second DUI offense, states such as Tennessee have a law that says the state can take the vehicle from you.

Rehabilitation. If you are found guilty of DUI you may have to go through a driver improvement program. Many states also make you go through a local alcohol or drug rehabilitation program to help you straighten out your drug problem.

Probation. Instead of jail time, some states put you on probation from one to three years. A probation officer checks with your family, school, and job to make sure you are staying sober. And you have to report to your probation officer at specific times.

License revocation. Getting a driver's license feels like the beginning of adult freedom. But it's also the beginning of adult responsibility. If you are convicted of DUI, you lose your license for at least a few months and possibly as long as a year. You give up the freedom because you abused your responsibility.

The federal government is becoming ever more concerned about drugs and driving. A new bill authorizes states to take away your driver's license if you are convicted of any drug offense, not just DUI.

Money problems. You may be surprised to find out how much it costs to fight a DUI arrest and court procedure in addition to the fines you'll have to pay.

Job loss. If your employer can't rely on you to get to work, you may lose your job. Getting a new job may be hard, too. Some job applications ask if you've ever been convicted of a crime. DUI is a crime.

Each state has its own laws against drunk and drugged driving. Check with the police department, motor vehicle bureau, or your driver's education teacher for the laws in your state. It is important to know what you risk if you get behind the wheel after using drugs.

From 1985 to 1995 the number of crashes and deaths from DUI fell, probably because the number of arrests and convictions had gone up. But in 1995, there was a slight increase in crashes and deaths due to DUI.

In an accident situation, fractions of a second in reaction time can mean the difference between life and death.

CHAPTER 7

Tragic Results

*I*f you use drugs and then get behind the wheel, the consequences can be fatal. You can kill innocent people, your own friends, or yourself.

Marina wanted to have a good time. She met several of her friends from school at a party. When one of them arrived with a six-pack of beer, they all began drinking.

Later that evening, Marina began to feel dizzy. Even though she was usually shy, she felt relaxed that night. She saw that some of her friends were smoking a joint. She sat next to them and took a long hit. It made her cough. Everyone laughed, but she didn't care. When the joint got passed to her again, she inhaled the smoke.

50 *Before she knew it, it was past 1 AM. "Oh, no!" she said, jumping to her feet. Marina's parents were going to kill her— she was over an hour late for her curfew. She looked around the room to find that most of her friends had either left the party or fallen asleep on the floor.*

Outside, she got into her car and headed home. Behind the wheel, Marina started to feel sleepy. Her eyelids felt heavy, and she could barely keep her eyes on the road. Suddenly, a car backed out of a driveway. Before she knew what was happening, Marina crashed right into it.

• Laurie was a passenger in a car driven by her friend. A daytime wine party ended in a crash into a telephone pole. Laurie's leg was crushed. Her college scholarship for track was gone.

• Jess is paralyzed from the waist down, the result of an almost lethal combination of cocaine and his motorcycle. "I didn't think I was too high to drive. I felt like I was smooth."

• Randi was a straight-A student and president of her senior class. A 17-year-old driver changed her life forever. Serious injuries from a car accident left

Randi a paraplegic with contracted and spastic hands and feet. She will never leave her wheelchair. Randi was the innocent victim of another person's bad decisions.

Maybe you know someone who has been in an accident while drunk or high on drugs. Maybe someone at your school, in your family, or in your neighborhood was killed in a car crash. You can read stories about it, but until you've actually seen it affect someone in your life, it's hard to believe that people you know can get into fatal accidents.

In October many high schools throughout America celebrate Red Ribbon Week. In 1993, using the slogan, "The Choice for Me Is Drug-Free," students and faculty got together to try to make the drugged driving problem seem more real. The observance was in memory of Enrique Camarena, a United States drug agent who was murdered by drug traffickers in 1985.

In order to impress upon young people the fact that fatal accidents really happen, some schools celebrating Red Ribbon Week stages mock wrecks. While school was in session, a car crash was staged in

52 | the parking lot. A few students volunteers to be "victims" in the crash. When everyone got out of school in the afternoon, they were shocked to find police, ambulances, two wrecked cars, and the "dead" bodies of five of their fellow students trapped inside the cars.

The mock wrecks opened the eyes of some people. "It's totally different when you see someone you know get killed," said Terry, a junior at one of the schools. "It's not just your parents and your teachers telling you not to use drugs and drive. It makes you think about how it could have been your best friend or your boyfriend who got killed."

CHAPTER 8

What You Can Do

"**M**y brother and his girlfriend had an accident coming home from a party," said Danielle, 15. "Todd was high and ran a stop sign. They crashed into another car. His girlfriend was thrown from the car and died. I've seen what he's going through. I don't want something like that to happen to me."

Danielle, with the help of a teacher at her school, started a **SAFE** program. SAFE stands for Substance Abuse Free Environment. The kids run promotions about staying straight, sober, and safe in situations where alcohol and other drugs threaten their well-being. Here are some other things you can do to protect the lives of the people in your community.

54 ## *Project Graduation*

Project Graduation is a national alcohol and safety program designed to keep kids safe, healthy, and alive during prom and graduation time.

Participants try to:
- Have teens sign pledges not to drink or do drugs and drive.
- Set up a Safe Ride system.
- Promote a "Buckle-Up Day."

SADD

Students Against Drunk Driving are groups of high school students who want to do something about the deadly combination of drinking and driving. In 1981, Robert Anatas, Director of Health Education in the Wayland Public Schools in Massachusetts, organized the program in his schools. The idea spread quickly.

Contract with Parents

In this SADD Program, teens and parents sign a contract where they both agree to be responsible for the teen's safety. The teen agrees that he or she will always ride with a sober driver and buckle his or her seat belt. If teens are in dangerous situations, they also agree to contact their parents to pick them up. The parent agrees

"Parent taxis" provide volunteer adults to drive teens to and from parties or proms.

56 | that he or she will pick up the teen at any time, day or night, no questions asked.

Safe Rides for Teens

Many schools have a Safe Rides program. If you or your ride home is drunk, you can call Safe Rides for a trip home. It is usually run by students, parents, teachers, and other volunteers. If you don't have a Safe Rides program at your school, speak with your teacher or principal to get one started. You might also ask a service organization in your town to work with you on the project.

Rent-a-Limo

When figuring out expenses for the junior and senior prom, many families add in the cost of renting a limousine for the evening.

"Our parents didn't want to worry about who was driving or what shape we were in," said Brett, 18. "So four couples and our parents chipped in and rented a limo for the prom. It was pretty cool!"

Radio and Media Announcements

Radio and TV stations often agree to give teens air time to pitch responsible messages. Announcements for staying sober are likely to make it on the air.

Contests

Take your message to middle and elementary schools by running slogan and poster contests. Ask local businesses to donate prizes for the kids to make a commitment to staying straight, sober, and safe.

Be sure you are organized before you try to sell this idea to your school. Giving a responsible presentation will get you respect and the approval to go ahead.

Organize a Rally

Put on an assembly with speakers who have had drunk driving tragedies or schoolmates who have lost a friend or relative to drugs and driving. Plan for the police or safety commission to do a car-crash demonstration. Have a persuasive speaker get the kids to take a pledge to stand up for their own lives and the right to be safe when they drive.

Peer Counseling

Peer counseling means kids helping kids. It uses students as role models, helpers, and leaders. Pairing up older, responsible teens with younger ones who need help, information, a contact, or a good influence is usually successful.

Obeying important safety rules is part of being a responsible driver.

Do you sometimes feel that you have no power, that you can't change the world? "I'm only one kid. What can I do?"

There's lots you can do right in your own little corner of the world. Working on a SADD organization, helping kids get safe rides, and being a role model can all make a difference.

It can save a life, including your own.

Glossary—
Explaining New Words

alcoholic Of or containing alcohol; a
person suffering from alcoholism.

anesthetic Drug used in medicine to
numb the sense of feeling.

barbiturate Any of various drugs used
to make one sleep.

consequence Result or outcome.

euphoric Feeling relaxed, happy.

felony A serious crime.

flashback A hallucination that occurs
long after the initial effects of a
drug have stopped.

hallucinogen Drug or chemical that
causes hallucinations or distorted
experiences.

inhibition Feelings that hold back
certain behaviors.

intoxication Loss of control of oneself
by use of alcohol or other drugs.

manslaughter The killing of a person
without previous intent to do so.

60 **marijuana** The dried leaves and flowers of the hemp plant; a drug that is smoked.

narcotic A drug such as morphine or heroin that dulls one's feelings and may lessen pain.

rehabilitation Process of bringing back to a normal or good condition.

sedative Tending to calm.

solvent Substance that can dissolve another.

stimulant A drug that excites or quickens the body's functioning.

Where to Go for Help

Center for Substance
  Abuse Prevention
(800) 662-HELP

Mothers Against Drunk
  Driving (MADD)
P.O. Box 541688
Dallas, TX 75354-1688
(800) 438-MADD
Web site: http://www.
  gran-net.com/madd.
  madd.html
e-mail: madd-
  national@ gran-
  net.com

Narcotics Anonymous
  (NA)
P.O. Box 9999
Van Nuys, CA 91409
(818) 773-9999

National Council on
  Alcoholism and Drug
  Dependence (NCADD)
12 West 21st Street
New York, NY 10010
(800) 622-2255
Web site: http://www.
  ncadd.org/
e-mail: national@
  NCADD.org

Students Against
  Drunk Driving
  (SADD)
P.O. Box 800
Marlboro, MA 01752
(508) 481-3568

In Canada

Alcoholics Anonymous
#202 Intergroup Office
234 Ellington Avenue E.
Toronto, ON M4P 1K5
(416) 487-5591

Mothers Against Drunk
  Driving (MADD)
  National Office
6507C Missauga Road
Missauga, ON L5N 1A6
(800) 665-6233

Narcotics Anonymous
P.O. Box 7500
Station A
Toronto, ON M5W 1P9
(416) 691-9519

For Further Reading

Adint, Victor. *Drugs and Prison.* New York: Rosen Publishing Group, Inc., 1995.

Dupont, Robert. *Getting Tough on Gateway Drugs.* Washington, DC: American Psychiatric Press, 1984.

Edwards, Gabrielle I. *Coping with Drug Abuse,* rev. ed. New York: Rosen Publishing Group, Inc., 1990.

Grosshandler, Janet. *Coping with Drinking and Driving,* rev. ed. New York: Rosen Publishing Group, Inc., 1997.

Plant, Martin & Moira Plant. *Risk-Takers: Alcohol, Drugs, Sex, and Youth.* New York: Routledge, 1992.

Taylor, Barbara. *Everything You Need to Know About Alcohol.* New York: Rosen Publishing Group, Inc., 1996.

Vogler, Roger E. & Wane R. Bartz. *Teenagers & Alcohol: When Saying No Isn't Enough.* Philadelphia: Charles Press, 1992.

Index

A

acid, 21
alcohol, 12, 14, 15, 16,
    18–19, 20, 29, 30, 33,
    35, 36, 38, 39, 41, 44,
    45
amphetamines, 12, 22, 45
angel dust, 20

B

barbiturates, 12, 28, 36
blood-alcohol content
    (BAC), 38
Breathalyzer, 44

C

Camarena, Enrique, 51
cocaine, 12, 24, 30, 45, 50
codeine, 45
community service, 9
conviction, 45
crack, 12, 24

D

Demerol, 27
depressants, 45
driving under the influence
    (DUI), 12, 15, 42
    arrest and conviction of,
        13, 14, 42–47
    financial costs of, 13
    laws about, 42–47
driving while intoxicated
    (DWI), 42

drugged driving
    aftermath of, 13
    teenagers dying from, 14,
        15
    what to do about, 53–58
Drug Recognition test,
    44–45
drugs, effects on driving
    ability, 12–13, 35–41

E

eye focus, 38

H

hallucinogens, 19–22, 45
hashish, 45
heroin, 27, 45

I

impairment, legal, 44
inhalants, 45
intoxication, 44

L

license revocation, 46
LSD, 21, 30, 45

M

marijuana, 8, 12, 19, 30, 45
    effects of, 19
    other names for, 19
morphine, 27

64

N
narcotics, 27, 45
nicotine, 22
night vision, 39

O
opium, 27
over-the-counter medicines,
    12

P
PCP (phencyclidine), 20–21,
    45
peripheral vision, 38
probation, 46
Project Graduation, 54

R
reaction time, 15, 36
Red Ribbon Week, 51–52
rehabilitation, 46

S
SADD, 54, 58
SAFE program, 53
Safe Ride, 54, 56
sedatives, 28
solvents, 24–25, 27
statistics
    on drunk and drugged
        drivers, 11, 13, 14–15,
        34, 47
    of high school students,
        16–18, 29–34
    leading causes of death,
        14
stimulants, 22, 45

T
THC, 19
time-sharing skill, 39

W
wreck, mock, 52

About the Author

Janet Grosshandler is a guidance counselor at Jackson Memorial High School, Jackson, New Jersey.

She earned a B.A. at Trenton State College in New Jersey and followed soon after with an M.Ed. from Trenton while teaching seventh-grade English.

Coping with Verbal Abuse, Coping with Drinking and Driving, Coping with Alcohol Abuse, and *The Value of Generosity* are other books by Janet and published by the Rosen Publishing Group.

Janet lives with her husband and three sons Nate, Jeff, and Mike in New Jersey. She makes time for running and reading.

Photo Credits
Cover by Stuart Rabinowitz; photos on pp. 2, 43 © AP/ Wide World Photos; all other photos by Stuart Rabinowitz.

DATE DUE

363.12
Gro   Grosshandler, Janet
Drugs and driving